# The Child with Autism
## Goes to Town

LABOSH
BOOKLETS

Look for additional Labosh Booklets in
# The Child with Autism Series

Children with autism and their parents deserve this insightful collection of suggestions and ideas about going out in public.

—Marlene Coleman M.D.
Pediatrics & Adolescent Medicine; author of
SAFE AND SOUND: HEALTHY TRAVEL WITH CHILDREN

# The Child with Autism
# Goes to Town

## The Go Anywhere Guide
### 250 tips for community outings

A part of the Child with Autism series

LABOSH
BOOKLETS

# Kathy Labosh

www.laboshpublishing.com

# LABOSH
## PUBLISHING

THE CHILD WITH AUTISM GOES TO TOWN
by Kathy Labosh
Published by Labosh Publishing
A part of the CHILD WITH AUTISM series of booklets
PO Box 588, East Petersburg, PA 17520-0588
www.laboshpublishing.com
email: info@laboshpublishing .com

Disclaimer: Please note that the materials contained in this
booklet are based on the author's own experiences and are
for informational purposes only. The reader is advised to use
his or her own judgement in applying the information to the
reader's own situation.

Cover and Interior Book Design by Pneuma Books, LLC
For more info, visit www. pneumabooks.com

Printed in the United States on acid-free paper by UGI

09 08 07 06 05     6 5 4 3 2

ISBN-13: 978-0-9744341-1-7
ISBN-10: 0-9744341-1-6
LCCN 2004091084

---

This booklet and all Labosh Booklets are available in quan-
tity discount for distribution and premium offers. If you are
an association, organization, corporation, or individual and
you would like to partner with Labosh Publishing to help people with autism and their loved ones, please contact Labosh
Publishing at partner@laboshpublishing.com or ask your
local autism support group to carry Labosh Booklets. Labosh
Booklets are available directly from Labosh Publishing or
through your major wholesaler. If you would like to create
a custom Labosh Booklet, please contact Labosh Publishing
directly. Thank you for your support.

This booklet
is dedicated to
Amy G. Hess...

Thanks for the road trips

# Table of Contents

# Foreword

## Richard Barbour

M.S., M.Ed.
Supervisor; Autism Support
Lancaster / Lebanon, PA IU 13

I have known Kathy and Timothy Labosh and their son Nicky, who is a student in the program under my supervision, for a year and a half. During that time I have been impressed with Kathy's determination, her sensitivity and insight, and her ability to share practical and helpful information, based on real-life experiences, to families and professionals alike.

I believe you will find this booklet useful. It is written with understanding. It is written with empathy. It is from the heart. The non-technical down-to-earth style is direct, and the tips offered incorporate an in-depth knowledge of how children with autism learn. It respects the child and affirms each child's own learning style and uniqueness.

This is a booklet that can be appreciated by families, professionals, and community providers. It not only affirms the right of all individuals to have access to their commu-

**The Child with Autism Goes to Town**

nities but also illustrates how this can be done so all can benefit.

—Richard Barbour, M.S., M.Ed.
Supervisor - Autism Support
Lancaster / Lebanon PA IU 13

# Preface

## Kathy Labosh

This booklet was written out of empathy for families living with autism. I do mean families. A particular child may have the symptoms, but the entire family is affected. In my own case, both of my children — Sam, age eleven and Nicky, age eight — have autism to varying degrees. I do not know what it is like to raise a typical child.

Over the years, I have learned many tricks for taking my children out into the community. Much of the wisdom contained in this book was gained by my own trial and error. Some tips are things I have learned in hindsight; others come from professionals who work with children with autism. My desire is for these tips to serve as trail markers for you as you venture out into the community with your child in tow.

Sam, our older son, is high-functioning and has always been a joy. Previously, I had credited this to my parenting skills. Then I had Nicky, who is low-functioning and prone to

# The Child with Autism Goes to Town

destroying things. Some children are more difficult than others. If your child is difficult, there are things you can do to improve his behavior in the community.

This booklet's roots go back to a time when I felt despair. Despite an early diagnosis and early treatment, Nicky was doing poorly in his Autism Early Intervention Class. Skills that he mastered one day would be forgotten the next.

In the fall of 2000, I got a glimpse into how Nicky learned best. I took my sons down to Emmitsburg, Maryland to see the autumn colors. We stopped at a mountainside shrine, and Nicky jumped out of the car and raced a half-mile to where there was a statue with a fountain and a pool. I was dumbfounded. We had been there only once, five months earlier, and Nicky had remembered the location of the fountain after seeing only the parking lot.

A few weeks later, I visited a friend I had not seen in years. She lived in a townhouse in a row of identical houses. Nicky ran to the correct townhouse, hurried up the steps, and went straight to the trampoline he remembered. My son, who knew only a few words receptively and could speak none, had a phenomenal memory for where he had been and what he had done there.

I then did what some would consider un- thinkable. I dropped his classroom days down to three. Two days each week I took him out into the community and with the as- sistance of Amy Hess, Nicky's Therapeutic Staff Support, taught him how to behave. A good helper in these endeavors is price- less. Together we explored the grocery store, fast food restaurants, farms, zoos, and the shopping mall. We photographed many of the things he saw on those trips and gave the photos to his autism class. Nicky's re- ceptive language grew as he connected the words he heard with the pictures of what he remembered.

He still speaks no words as of 2004, but he has a maturity and a worldly savvy that al- lows him to handle many social situations. He is back in his autism class full-time and is now learning his academics. I firmly be- lieve his exposure to the community at large will aid in his learning for years to come.

Please note: the only time I could work with Nicky one-on-one was while his brother was in school. You need to evaluate what will work best for your family.

Most of the hints in this book were gleaned from those experiences. Sam, our older son, enjoys all the activities in this book as well. Nicky can now do everything but sit through a church service or a movie. Their behavior is not perfect but neither is the behavior of typical children.

Good luck in your endeavors. I pray this booklet helps your family enjoy a full and active life in the community.

—Kathy Labosh—
Labosh Publishing

## About the Author, Kathy Labosh

Kathy Labosh graduated from Penn State and worked as an economist. She is now a stay-at-home mom to Sam and Nicky, both of whom are children with autism. It became her mission to help others in similar situations. Kathy formed a Special Education Religion Class and is the author of a specialized curriculum for children with autism. She also received an Honorable Mention for Children's Fiction from Writer's Digest.

# Thank You

---

## Contributors and Consultants

Diane Boomsma, F.I.A.C.P.,
Registered Pharmacist

Peter J. Ross, D.M.D.,
Pediatric Dentist

Timothy Labosh, M.D.,
Family Practice Doctor

LaNita Miller, BCBA, MS, Sp. Ed.,
Special Education Teacher

---

Thank you to Sam and Nicky Labosh. Your smiling faces and loving hearts have made me the happiest of mothers.

# 1
# The Playground

The playground is the easiest social outing. The main obstacles are interaction with other children and the physical skills necessary to master the equipment. The playground is a good first step toward social interaction. The child with autism will observe typical play and feel little or no pressure to join.

❶ Go to the playground when it is not crowded. Your child will have a chance to explore the area with few social interactions and less sensory stimuli. After your child is comfortable at the playground, go at busier times.

❷ Use the little children's swings to hold your child securely while he learns to hold on and gets used to the swinging sensation. When it is evident that he enjoys the swinging motion, move to the regular swings.

❸ Swing gently on the regular swings until your child consistently holds on.

❹ Teach the pumping motion when your

1

child is still. Hold his legs out in front and say, "Front." Push his legs back and say, "Back."

❺ Demonstrate the pumping motion while saying, "Front" and "Back."

❻ Push your child on the swings saying, "Front" and "Back." The pumping motion takes a long time to learn, but persist, and make it fun.

❼ Stop the teaching exercise and swing as usual if your child gets stressed. The focus should be on his having fun outside the home.

❽ Go down a wide, straight slide with your child. Hold him between your legs and say, "That was fun!" Do this several times.

❾ Go down the slide first and then encourage your child to come to you.

❿ Start with a small slide. A child with autism goes down a ladder facing outward, which can be dangerous.

⓫ Teach your child how to back down a ladder. Have a helper go up the ladder first and stop at the top. Your child will go up next. You stay behind your child. To start back down, pick up your child's foot and put it on the

# ❸ The Playground

lower bar. The helper should then back down also, forcing your child to descend. Praise your child with each step he retreats. Reward your child when he has reached the bottom.

⓬ Do not go up the ladder if your child is descending facing outward. He may jump into your arms or hug you. This could tip you over backward. Stay at the bottom of the ladder with your feet firmly on the ground ready to catch your child should he fall.

⓭ Remember what your child is wearing before you enter a fun fort. It is easy to lose a child in the wooden structures.

⓮ Stay in visual contact with your child. Even if the playground has only one entrance, park benches are often placed against the walls. A child could easily exit without you knowing.

⓯ Bring snacks and drinks for your child. Other children's food is often in plain sight and can be a great temptation.

# 2
# The Fast-Food Restaurant

Being able to eat at a fast food restaurant as a family is essential if you are ever going to leave the house for more than a day trip. The obstacles you need to overcome are finding a food your child will eat, keeping him at the table, and teaching him to wait in a line for his food. The fast food restaurant can be an excellent place to perfect his eating-out manners. You have much more control in getting your food at a fast food restaurant. You won't stick out as much as you might think, because typical children do not always behave in fast food restaurants either.

❶ Go through the drive-thru and eat at home. Find out what your child likes to eat, so he has motivation for staying in the restaurant later.

❷ Go through the drive-thru and eat in the restaurant during a non-busy time. This will give your child practice at staying at the table.

❸ Have your child sit in a booth close to a

window. Sit beside him so he can't get out except by climbing over you.

❹ Cut the burger into quarters if your child tends to separate his food into all the different components. He is less likely to separate a bite-size piece. It is also easier for you to hold if you need to encourage him to eat.

❺ Bring a special activity bag that your child gets to play with only at the restaurant.

❻ Bring a timer so your child knows how long he is expected to stay there.

❼ Have your child throw the trash in the proper receptacle.

❽ Go to the restaurant with another adult at a non-busy time when you are ready to practice waiting. This person will sit with your child at the table while you order food at the counter. Make sure he can see you in line.

❾ Go to the restaurant with your child at a non-busy time. Have him wait with you while you order your food. Go to the table with him.

❿ Move gradually to busier times. When your child is confident of where he is and what he is doing, he will be able to handle more people.

# The Child with Autism Goes to Town

⓫ Beware that an impulsive child may steal food off of other people's tables. Keep a watch especially when walking through the restaurant.

⓬ Practice ordering with your child. Let him give the order when he has it memorized.

⓭ Have your child give the money to the cashier. This will teach him that we exchange money for things we want.

⓮ Have a child that knows math calculate the change.

⓯ Order a pizza over the phone but eat it at the restaurant. Have your child watch the workers making pizzas while you eat.

⓰ Order at the pizza parlor and sit where your child can see the food being made while you wait. Be sure to bring his special activity bag.

⓱ Move to other fast-serving establishments. Explain that the food is being made behind the wall. Hopefully by this time, your child understands that the food will come.

⓲ Order mild General Tso's chicken as a good first meal from a Chinese restaurant.

# 3

# The Mall

Shopping at the mall is a difficult but necessary skill that a child with autism needs to master if he is going to function in society. The main obstacles are coping with the sensory overload of so many sights, sounds, smells, and people; staying with the family; and learning not to handle the merchandise. It is better to teach this in a store where you can buy what he breaks than in a friend's home when he's broken another child's trophy.

❶ Attach a dog tag with your child's name, your name, your phone number, and the word "AUTISM" to the inner laces of your child's shoe. This is particularly helpful if the child is non-verbal. If you carry a cell phone with you all of the time, use that phone number. I might be reluctant to write your address where predators could see it.

❷ Write out a script for your child. "Who are you?" "Sam Labosh." "What's your phone number?" "555-5555." A child with autism will do better if he can see it written out.

# The Child with Autism Goes to Town

Practice these questions and answers at home.

❸ Go early when the mall is open but the stores are not. It is usually open for walkers who want to exercise.

❹ Walk around the mall to familiarize your child with the building. Make a note of what is of particular interest to your child.

❺ Expect to spend long periods of time going up and down escalators and stairs.

❻ Bring small pieces of candy. Give your child a reward for staying with you over a certain distance. Praise lavishly.

❼ Buy your child a snack when the stores open and then go home.

❽ Have your child try the coin-operated rides.

❾ Go into a clothing store or another store where the objects are hard to break. Tell your child, "No touch," if he tries to grab something. Keep practicing over time until he gets the idea.

❿ Stay longer and longer at the mall.

⓫ Buy shoes at stores that let you pick out

the shoes from boxes instead of having to wait for a shoe salesman.

⓬ Bring a helper to keep track of your child while you look at merchandise for an actual shopping trip or until you are confident that he will stay with you.

# 4
# The Barber or Hairdresser

The child with autism hates getting his hair cut, but a well-groomed appearance can aid greatly in social acceptance. The main obstacles are the child's oversensitivity to his hair being touched, the noisy clippers, and the long time the child must sit still. Mastering these skills will be useful in other social situations.

❶ Play with your child's hair. Pull up on it and hold the hair the way the hairdresser or barber will. Smile at your child; make it an affectionate little game. Do not pull too hard.

❷ Buy clippers. Let your child feel the vibration on his hand and get used to the noise at home.

❸ Go to a kid's haircut place that shows videos.

❹ Make an appointment so that the wait time is not as long.

## ❹ The Barber or Hairdresser

❺ Do not get his hair washed at the salon until your child is already comfortable with the rest of the process.

❻ Explain to the hairdresser that your child has autism and that speed is important.

❼ Use a booster seat to hold your child more securely.

❽ Fill your child's hands with his favorite candy. He will have to drop his candy to grab the scissors.

❾ Hold your child in place and reassure him. Get below him if possible so he can see your face. Give him lots of praise.

❿ Give your child a reward afterward no matter how badly he did. You want him to associate this activity with a treat afterward. If you get angry, he will avoid this particular activity at all costs.

⓫ Get a haircut on a regular basis. The more familiar your child is with any situation, the better he will behave.

# 5

# The Grocery Store

Having your child behave in the grocery store can be one of the biggest stress reducers a parent can have. Even parents with typical children dread this trip. The most important skill your child needs to learn is to stay with the cart. It is a nightmare to try to keep track of him while getting something at the deli counter.

❶ Bring an assistant if you can when you first move your child out of the grocery cart and train him to walk beside it. This assistant should continually bring your child back to the cart.

❷ Have your child hold the push bar of the cart when you go solo. Put your arms around him on either side with your hands gripping the same bar. If he places his feet on the lower shelf of the cart, you can push the cart around like it's a ride.

❸ Raise one arm to let your child out and

help him pick up the food and place it in the cart.

❹ Go at a non-busy time to cut down on wait times when checking out.

❺ Go and pick up only a few items, including your child's favorite food. You want the trip to be short and your child's opportunity for success to be high.

❻ Get your child's favorite food first. Place it in the bottom center of the cart, in plain sight but out of reach. He will want to keep in close visual contact with that item.

❼ Bring a small candy treat to give your child when he has stayed with the cart for an entire aisle.

❽ Be liberal in praise.

❾ Tell your child he can pick out one treat. If he wants something else show him the first treat. Tell him, "We got this — you'll get the other next time." If he insists on the second item, get it, but put the first back.

❿ At the register, have your child help unload the groceries. As soon as the groceries are paid for, give him his treat and tell him what a good boy he is.

# The Child with Autism Goes to Town

**⓫** In time, the assistant won't be needed. Move to longer and longer lists.

**⓬** Make a learning project. Take photos of the food normally bought and make a pictorial list for your child. Have him go to that item in the store.

**⓭** Write the names on the back and use the photos as flashcards.

**⓮** Go into the self-scanning aisle if your child is older and have him practice putting items into the bag while you scan.

**⓯** Have an older child practice scanning items.

**⓰** A great deal of self-esteem can be raised mastering these tasks. As difficult as it may be to learn, a child with autism enjoys a task once he has mastered it.

# 6
# The Movie Theater

Going to a movie with a child with autism can seem like a pipe dream, but your child can learn to enjoy the experience. The main obstacles are fear of the dark, the noises, upsetting images, and sitting for a long time. I've always gone to nearly empty matinees during the training process, and the other people in the theater have always been fine with it. I was more concerned than they were.

❶ Have your child watch his favorite DVD or video in an increasingly dark room. You should start with all the lights on. Next eliminate the lights closest to the TV. Gradually reduce the lighting until there is only a small light at the back of the room.

❷ Tell your child that you are pretending to be in a theater. You should sit next to him and watch the video. Make it a fun time.

❸ Slowly turn up the volume as well. In movie theaters, the sound tends to be quite loud. Your child needs to be slowly acclimated to louder noises.

❹ Give your child popcorn to eat and his favorite drink while watching the video.

❺ Turn off the video if your child gets up and won't come back to his seat. Restart it when he returns and give him small pieces of his favorite candy over short intervals of time for staying in his seat. If he just won't sit, let it go. This is not the place for power struggles.

❻ Go to a local movie theater and explain that your child has autism and you would like him to see what a theater looks like inside. Let him look around. Tell him what everything is.

❼ Pick a very gentle movie — one that is not likely to have many loud noises or explosions. You may never get your child back in the theater if he is terrified early on.

❽ Take him to a matinee of the movie when the movie is on its way out. The theater will be practically empty.

❾ Go late to avoid the previews. Previews tend to show the most stimulating scenes, which can scare your child. Previews are often louder than the actual show.

❿ Buy your child a big tub of popcorn and place it on his lap.

⓫ Buy your child a soda.

⓬ Buy a large box of small candies. When the popcorn and soda run out, give the candy to your child for staying put.

⓭ Take your child to the bathroom if he wants to leave the theater. Ask him if he wants to go back in. If not, take him home and praise him for the time he stayed.

⓮ Expect to leave before the end of the show. It can take several tries before your child will sit through an entire movie.

# 7
# Church

Many parents deeply desire to pass their faith on to their child with autism. Often, this faith is what sustains the parents through the rough times. Even a non-verbal child can learn aspects of faith through visual means and hands-on activities.

❶ Say the basic prayers of your faith every night with your child at bedtime. Children with autism have good auditory memory, even if an understanding is lacking, and learn language in phrases. One day your child may surprise you by saying the whole prayer.

❷ Watch religious children's videos, such as VEGGIE TALES. Children with autism are visual learners and will remember videos.

❸ Have your child listen to religious songs. Many children remember words set to music better than when those same words are spoken.

18

❹ Let your child play with plastic statues or action figures of people important to your faith. Tell him their names and something about them. Plastic statues last longer than the action figures.

❺ Play a matching game with pictures of people important to your faith.

❻ Get simple books containing faith stories that have been passed down for generations. These stories connect your child culturally with others of your faith.

❼ Use felt boards to illustrate religious stories. Let your child place the people in the scene.

❽ Have them assemble religious-themed puzzles.

❾ Take photographs of everything in your house of worship. Cut the main object out of the photo and place it on a flashcard. Laminate the card.

❿ Write a social story about what happens during the service using the photos.

⓫ Let your child examine the church when no one is around. Whenever your child comes to an object that you've photographed, show him the photograph and repeat its name.

⓬ Give your child the photograph and have him go to the object.

⓭ Tell your child to go to the object. If he does not remember its name, show him the photograph. Let this be fun and games time.

⓮ Have your child sit in the narthex or lobby or sit in the cry room if it is not full of noisy children.

⓯ Have your child play with a quiet toy like a calculator during the service.

⓰ Sit up front where your child can see what is going on. It will also lessen the social anxiety if he doesn't see as many people.

⓱ Let your child follow along in the missal or program or bulletin.

⓲ Tell your child how long the service will take.

⓳ For Catholics, GLEA (God's Love Embraces Autism) has a pictorial social story of the Mass with the responses entitled, WE GO TO MASS. Contact Grace Harding at the Diocese of Pittsburgh (disabilities@diopitt.com) for information about GLEA and contact Silver

Burdett Ginn: Religion Titles at 1-800-552-2259 for the book.

❷⓿ The Rose Fitzgerald Kennedy Program to Improve Catholic Education for Children and Adults with Mental Retardation provides twelve years of religious education lesson plans. It was written by the Diocese of Pittsburgh and produced by The Joseph P. Kennedy, Jr. Foundation. Copies of the book are currently available from Silver Burdett Ginn: Religion Titles for sixty-five dollars. Contact them at 1-800-552-2259.

❷❶ Start a small, religious education class in your church specifically for children with developmental disabilities. Use the Rose Kennedy Curriculum or THE CHILD WITH AUTISM LEARNS THE FAITH, which will be published by Labosh Publishing in 2005. Contact us at 1-717-898-3813, visit our website at www.laboshpublishing.com, or email us at laboshpublishing@msn.com.

# 8

# The Amusement Park

Going to an amusement park can eventually be a very enjoyable experience for children with autism, but at first the noises and crowds, can be overly stimulating. The main considerations are the wait time, the crowds, and which rides to choose.

❶ Make sure your child is already comfortable at the playground before trying an amusement park.

❷ Buy your tickets ahead of time. Tickets are usually available at a discount at your local AAA. They are often available with special promotions at the local grocery stores or drug stores as well. This will cut down on the wait to get in once you get to the park.

❸ Go during a weekend in the spring or fall the first time you go. The park is usually less crowded. When your child is comfortable with the park you can go at busier times.

❹ Wear a fanny pack instead of a backpack

or purse. This gets you through security faster, and it leaves both hands free for your child. Have another member of the party carry other items and meet them inside.

❺ Go to Guest Relations. Explain that your child has autism and has difficulty waiting in line. Bring a doctor's note. Some parks require it and others don't. They will give you a pass that allows you quicker (though not immediate) access to the rides. The access is usually through the exit or the handicapped area. They will give you a brochure explaining the procedure for each ride.

❻ Take the card instead of the bracelet if a choice is offered. A child with touch sensitivities will not be able to tolerate a bracelet.

❼ Cut the bracelet with a key if your child is having a major breakdown. The bracelets are difficult to unsnap, and with security checks you will have no other sharp objects around.

❽ Start with the monorail if the park has one. It is a smooth ride and gives your child a good overall view of the park. You can point out various rides that you want to try.

❾ Sit with your arm around your child toward the back of the steam train. This will get you away from the steam engine's whistle and general noise.

**❿** Take the observation tower that slowly climbs into the air and then rotates to give your child another overview of the park.

**⓫** Sit with your child on the kiddie rides that go up in the air. These rides are early favorites for a child with autism.

**⓬** Try the Mini-Himalaya if the park has one. My son surprised me by putting his arms up in the air.

**⓭** Know your child before putting him on the spinning cups. If he tends to whirl repetitively he will love it. But some children are sensitive to the spinning motion.

**⓮** Have your child try the large slides with the burlap bags to sit on. My children rode them over and over again.

**⓯** Beware of the merry-go-round. It can overwhelm the senses of a child with autism. The music is loud. Part of the world around them (outside the merry-go-round) seems to be moving, but other parts around them seem to stay in the same spot. They are also being moved up and down while straddling an unfamiliar object. You need to take this slow.

**16** First sit on the bench seats that are usually found on merry-go-rounds. This cuts off part of the view and gets your child used to the music and the constantly changing view. You also have more control over your child, if there is a problem.

**17** Move to a stationary horse if the bench seat went well. This will get your child accustomed to balancing himself on a horse. If he tries to get off, it is easier to hold on to him.

**18** Go to a moving horse if the stationary horse went well. Stand on the outside of the horse. If your child decides to bolt, he will go to the outside, away from the carousel. You will be able to catch him and unbuckle the belt. If you are on the inside of the horse, the horse will be between you and your escaping child. If he manages to get his inside leg over the horse, he'll be hanging by the belt.

**19** Watch out for rides where you will get splashed. If your child does not like the shower, he will not like getting splashed and may try to escape.

**20** Bring a spare set of clothes for accidents or if your child's clothes get wet.

**21** Try putting your child under a hose sprin-

## The Child with Autism Goes to Town

kler or shower at home first, before putting
him on a ride where he will get splashed.

**㉒** Avoid dark, loud, or scary rides.

**㉓** Bring your child's favorite foods if he has
taste sensitivities. Otherwise, hamburgers,
cheeseburgers, hot dogs, and pizza are read-
ily available in the park.

# 9

# Sports & Sports Events

Sports are important to your child's social life at school. It is good to help your child participate, even as a spectator. Participating in sports builds self-confidence, improves motor coordination, and often builds social skills.

❶ Avoid large sporting events that can be noisy with little warning. Fans jumping up and screaming can be alarming to a child with autism. Open-ended stadiums are quieter than closed stadiums or indoor arenas.

❷ Start with minor league baseball games. The stadiums are smaller, quieter, and the activities are family oriented. They often offer fun activities for the children between every inning.

❸ Watch different sports on TV. See what sports appeal to your child.

❹ Visit a local children's soccer game. Let your child watch from the bleachers or walk around the sidelines to see what is going on.

## The Child with Autism Goes to Town

❺ Buy him sodas or bring his favorite foods.

❻ Check with Special Olympics or Easter Seals to see what sporting opportunities are available for children with disabilities.

❼ Ask your local pool about private swimming lessons. If you intend to go to a pool or the beach as a family, it is essential that your child learn enough swimming skills to be safe in the water.

❽ Buy a stationary bike and treadmill for the house. These are good for your child's physical fitness, but they can be dangerous and require constant supervision.

❾ Visit a roller-skating rink or ice-skating rink. Either enroll your child in private lessons or teach him yourself if you are proficient.

❿ Take your child to a local ski resort with an inner tube run. No experience is required.

⓫ Take your child skiing as long as you are proficient enough to control both you and your child. Have your child ski at your side as both of you hold your poles horizontally in front of you. Do this until your child learns the basic wedge position and learns to control his speed. This may take a long time.

# 10

# The Doctor

Doctor's visits can be difficult. The major obstacles are the wait time until you see the doctor, the occasional need for multiple shots, and all the fascinating objects in the examination room that your child should not touch.

❶ Apply for medical assistance. Children with autism are usually eligible regardless of their parents' income.

❷ Ask around the autism community to find a doctor experienced with autism. An experienced doctor is more likely to tolerate and understand your child's behavior. He or she will also be more current on the latest developments. In general, a younger doctor will likely know more about autism than an older doctor. Until recently, autism was considered so rare it was given little coverage in medical school curriculum. Even pediatricians were not previously well- informed.

❸ Look for a doctor that is flexible and has

## The Child with Autism Goes to Town

confidence in you as a parent. Children with autism exhibit unusual behaviors. If you think a particular treatment is helping a particular behavior, your doctor should trust your observations.

❹ Look for a doctor who will look at and talk to your child, even if your child is non-verbal. Avoid a doctor who talks only to you and ignores your child except when performing the physical examination.

❺ Bring your child to the doctor's office at a time when he doesn't have an appointment and the office is not crowded. Let him get familiar with the waiting area and if possible an exam room. A reasonable doctor experienced with autism would allow this.

❻ Read the child a social story about what happens at the doctor's office. Look for one that uses photographs and simple language.

❼ When you go to the appointment, bring an activity bag for long waits.

❽ Bring an extra adult, if you can, to look after your child's needs while you talk to the doctor.

❾ Ask the doctor to limit the initial physical exam to no more than absolutely necessary. For the first visit, the doctor might do no more with your child than talk and try to set your child at ease.

❿ Ask the nurse if they can hold off putting you in the room until just before the doctor gets there. The shorter the wait time, the smaller the chances are that your child will act out.

⓫ Let your child play with the water in the sink, if he gets bored with the activity bag.

⓬ Let your child leave the room with the other adult if the doctor is through with him but still needs to discuss something with you.

⓭ Ask for an additional nurse if your child is receiving multiple shots. They can be administered at the same time on both legs.

⓮ Give the shots last if possible, so you can leave quickly afterward.

⓯ Ask your doctor if you can give your child a mild sedative before a visit involving multiple shots or invasive procedures.

LABOSH
BOOKLETS

# 11
# The Pharmacy & Medicine

Getting traditional medicines down a child's throat can be difficult. Children with autism are not good at swallowing pills and are not easily persuaded to swallow anything they don't like. There are, however, some tricks to make it easier on your child and some new ways of dispensing medicine available from compounding pharmacists.

❶ See if the pill comes in a quick-dissolve tablet.

❷ Have a compounding pharmacist make the medicine into a flavored troche. Its texture is similar to a gummy bear.

❸ Secure the medicine carefully because your child may think it is candy.

❹ Have liquid medicine flavored by the pharmacist.

❺ Have a compounding pharmacist make the

32

medicine into a transdermal gel which can
be rubbed on the child's skin.

❻ Do not use medicine patches. Children
with autism often won't tolerate a patch or
even a Band-Aid on their skin.

❼ Have a compounding pharmacist make Al-
lithiamine into a gel that can be rubbed on
the soles of the child's feet. Warning — it
smells like garlic.

❽ Have a compounding pharmacist make Se-
cretin into a frozen gel that can be rubbed on
the child's wrists.

❾ Some drug stores deliver medicines that
need to be compounded; it can save an extra
trip to the pharmacy.

❿ Hide regular pills in chunky peanut but-
ter. Your child will have a hard time distin-
guishing the pill from the peanuts. (Do not
do this if your child has peanut allergies.)

⓫ Place your child's chin in the palm of your
hand, lift his head up, and blow in his face.
This forces him to swallow. Do this if your
child tends to spit out medicine.

⓬ Give your child chocolate to eat before giving him a bitter-tasting medicine. Its strong
flavor masks bitter flavors.

# The Child with Autism Goes to Town

**⑬** Give your child yogurt or milk products before giving him medicine. Milk coats the tongue and throat, so your child will not taste the medicine as much. (Not for those children on a dairy-free diet.)

**⑭** Have a favorite candy treat in sight and ready to give when your child has to take a bitter-tasting medicine.

**⑮** Mix liquid medicine with Kool-Aid. Juice works quite well with some medicines but not with others because of its acidic nature.

**⑯** Sprinkle powders over ice cream with nuts. (This method is not for children with nut allergies or who are on a dairy-free diet.)

**⑰** Mix powders in applesauce.

**⑱** Mix powders in yogurt. (Not for those on a dairy-free diet.)

**⑲** ALL medicines should be taken on a trial basis. Some cold medications can make children hyperactive; some will instead cause drowsiness. Other medications make children with autism aggressive. Watch carefully for side effects. Discontinue over-the-counter medicine if the side effects are worse than the symptoms being treated. With prescription medicines, call your doctor to report side effects.

# The Dentist

## 12

Good dental care is important. A big obstacle can be our own childhood memories of the dentist. Dentistry has changed. Advances in equipment and techniques make the process less painful. Pediatric dentists create a child-friendly environment.

❶ Find a pediatric dentist. They have the most experience with children with developmental delays.

❷ Take your child to the waiting room when he does not have an appointment. Let him explore the waiting area and then go home.

❸ Make a list of your child's favorite DVDs. Many offices play movies for the patients. It is good to have a suggestion of an alternate movie if your child dislikes the one that is being shown.

❹ Read a social story with photographs about going to the dentist.

# The Child with Autism Goes to Town

❺ Bring some of your child's favorite toys to distract him from the dental exam.

❻ In the first few visits, the dentist will often just look in your child's mouth and touch his teeth and then do a gentle brushing.

❼ Tell your child that the dentist is counting his teeth. Many children with autism count everything, and counting teeth will make perfect sense.

❽ Children with autism may benefit from several visits to the dental office to acclimate to the office routines, sounds, smells, and people.

❾ Have your child observe a cooperative child during a non-invasive dental appointment. This only works if your child has an interest in what others are doing.

❿ Have your child practice opening his mouth at home. After a small wait, pop a candy in his mouth.

⓫ Have your child practice opening his mouth and put in a Popsicle stick. Move it around like the dentist might. Give your child a reward.

⓬ Have your child practice spitting by having a spitting contest at the sink. Your child will love this.

❸ The first time your child goes for a real cleaning, use a mild sedative until he gets used to the routine. Consult with your dentist.

❹ Be in the treatment room with your child to assist the dentist by keeping your child's hands away from the dentist and the instruments in your child's mouth.

❺ Give the dentist an opportunity to talk to your child. Your child may be more cooperative with a friendly dentist who looks at him while talking to him.

❻ Check to see if your child's dental surgery can be done in the hospital under general anesthesia. Insurance will usually pay if the dentist submits a letter of medical necessity. Dental insurance usually doesn't cover anesthesia unless there was an accident, but Medical Assistance often will, even if the dentist doing the work doesn't accept Medical Assistance.

❼ Use nitrous oxide if your child can handle getting dental work done in the office.

# 13
# The Hospital

Hopefully if your child needs to go to the hospital, there will be time to prepare your child for the experience. Your role is to be an intermediary — helping the medical staff and your child understand each other.

❶ Inform the medical staff that your child has autism. Explain the degree to which the autism affects your child's ability to communicate and follow instructions.

❷ Tell them your child will rip the IV out of his arm if he gets the chance.

❸ Ask them to pre-sedate your child prior to inserting any IV or giving anesthesia.

❹ Bring a small blanket or afghan to place on the floor. As the sedative takes effect, your child will become unsteady on his feet and should be encouraged to play on the floor.

❺ Call the unit working with your child, for example — the Day Surgery Unit, and explain that your child has trouble with long waits. Ask them to estimate the time they will actually start to work with your child.

❻ Take your child for a walk around the hospital and waiting area to familiarize him with the hospital.

❼ Ask if there are any forms that you can fill out ahead of time.

❽ Bring another adult with you to attend to your child while you are talking with the hospital personnel.

❾ Bring an activity bag. (No food if there will be general anesthesia.) Make it as fun a wait as possible.

❿ Try not to be anxious. Your child will not be calmer than you are.

⓫ When your child starts coming out of the anesthesia, he will immediately grab for the IV. Keep a close eye on him to make sure he doesn't harm himself trying to rip it out of his arm.

⓬ In the pediatric ward, check to see what movies are available and pick a favorite.

⓭ Have someone your child knows stay with him the entire time — of course, a parent is always best.

# 14
# The Library

Whether you actually take your child to the library or not depends greatly upon your child. I have not taken Nicky to the library, because like many children with autism he loves the sound of ripping paper. He is also noisy despite being non-verbal. We do, however, have a tremendous number of children's books at home. Most children's books are not suitable because children with autism do not understand language and cannot look at a picture and determine what is important.

Below is a list of children's publishers and authors whose books are most suitable for children with autism and a list of catalogs with their websites for books made specifically for the child with autism.

❶ Most picture books by DK Publishers are useful for building vocabulary, but they often have too many pictures on a page for a child with autism. It is often difficult for them to focus on a particular one. Use their smaller books.

❷ Scholastic has a series of Big Photo Books

❸ Jennifer Armstrong's books, especially SUNSHINE, MOONSHINE

❹ Stan and Jan Berenstain's early reader books especially BIG BEAR, SMALL BEAR

❺ Sandra Boynton's Board Books

❻ Norman Bridwell's Clifford series

❼ Helen Oxenburg's books especially I SEE, I HEAR, I TOUCH

❽ Molly Coxe's books especially BIG EGG

❾ P. D. Eastman's books especially GO,DOG. GO!

❿ Max Haynes' book TICKLEMONSTER AND ME is the best interactive play book. Our son Sam wanted us to read this together a couple of times every night for months.

⓫ Yvonne Hooker's English translation of ONE GREEN FROG

⓬ Mercer Mayer's book A BOY, A DOG AND A FROG

⓭ Peggy Rothmann's book GOOD NIGHT GORILLA

# The Child with Autism Goes to Town

❶❹ Richard Scarry's book WATCH YOUR STEP, MR. RABBIT! This is good if you demonstrate push, pull, and blow with your child while reading. Children enjoy the interaction. Mr. Scarry's word books have pictures that are too complicated for a child with autism to focus on a particular object.

❶❺ Dr. Seuss' book HOP ON POP. Dr. Seuss' other books can get too complicated very quickly. If your child is high functioning you can try them.

# 15
# Family Gatherings

Family gatherings can be the most difficult of trips. The main challenges will be expectations about how you and your child should behave, houses that are not child-proofed, and the high level of social interaction directed at your child. Children with taste sensitivities may also not like any of the food prepared.

❶ Travel, if possible, in two cars. One parent can return home with your child if he gets distressed and the rest of the family can stay.

❷ Feed your child ahead of time. A fed child is better behaved than a hungry one.

❸ Allay concerns that your child doesn't eat enough by explaining that he already ate.

❹ Bring food that your child will eat.

❺ Feed your child in a separate room, if he was not fed ahead of time.

# The Child with Autism Goes to Town

**❻** Come early before most of the people arrive. This lets your child get accustomed to the growing number of people rather than being plunged into a noisy crowd.

**❼** Ask if you can remove certain breakables from your child's reach. If the host believes you should just teach him not to touch things, explain that your child's brain development has been affected. People accommodate the blind and the deaf. Autism is not a result of bad parenting; it is a physical disability that can only be partially overcome by extensive therapy.

**❽** Avoid homes where people refuse to accommodate by doing even the simplest of child-proofing. This creates an inappropriate stress level on you and your child. They can visit you at your house.

**❾** Pick a quiet place to go if your child becomes distressed.

**❿** Bring your child's favorite toys or stuffed animals.

**⓫** Show your child individual pictures of family members and teach him their names.

**⓬** Write out simple courtesy phrases and responses to questions. "How are you?" "I am fine." "How is school?" "Good." Rehearse before you go.

⓭ Take your child out for a walk if he gets distressed.

⓮ Avoid the consumption of too much chocolate. They get hyperactive with the sugar and then emotionally fragile when their blood sugar level drops. Let them have cookies or other less sugary treats instead.

⓯ Dress your child nicely. Forgiveness comes easier to kids who look cute.

⓰ Let others watch your child if they volunteer. You need the break.

⓱ Ask for help if you need it. People cannot read minds or anticipate your needs. Most people are glad to help if they are asked to do a specific task. "Please help me," is too general a statement. "Could you watch him while I eat?" is specific.

⓲ Treasure any positive comments.

⓳ Accept unwanted advice with the phrase, "I'll have to think about that," and smile. They really are trying to help. People cannot understand what it is like to live with autism until they experience it for themselves.

# Resources

**16**

---

**Children's Books & Other Materials**

Children's books, teaching tools, and information about autism can be found in the following catalogs and websites:

❶ "Abilitations" – Call 1-800-850-8602 or visit www.abilitations.com.

❷ Autism-Aspergers Publishing Co. – Call 1-913-897-1004 or visit www.asperger.net.

❸ "Beyond Play" – Call 1-877-428-1244 or visit www.beyondplay.com.

❹ "Different Roads to Learning" – Call 1-800-853-1057 or visit www.difflearn.com.

❺ Future Horizons, Inc. – Call 1-800-489-0727 or visit www.FutureHorizons-autism.com.

❻ Jessica Kingsley Publications – Call 011-442-078332301 or visit.jkp.com.

❼ Labosh Publishing – Call 1-717-898-3813 or visit www.laboshpublishing.com.

❽ Mayer-Johnson Co. – Call 1-800-588-4548 or visit www.mayer-johnson.com.

❾ Phat Art 4 – Call 1-866-250-9798 or visit www.phatart4.com.

❿ "Pocket Full of Therapy" – Call 1-732-462-5888 or visit www.pfot.com.

⓫ "Special Needs Project" – Call 1-800-333-6867 or visit www.specialneeds.com.

⓬ Super Duper Publications – Call 1-800-277-8737 or visit www.superduperinc.com.

⓭ The Center for Speech and Language Disorders – Call 1-630-530-8551 or visit www.csld.com.

⓮ Woodbine House – Call 1-800-843-7323 or visit www.woodbinehouse.com.

---

## Autism Resources

The ARC of the United States – Call 1-301-565-3842 or visit www.thearc.org.

Autism Research Institute – Fax 1-619-563-6840 or visit www.autism.com.

# The Child with Autism Goes to Town

Autism Society of America — Call 1-800-3AUTISM or visit www.autism-society.org.

Bubel/Aiken Foundation — Call 1-224-430-0950 or visit www.thebubelaikenfoundation.org/home.htm.

Doug Flutie Jr. Foundation — Call 1-866-3AUTISM or visit www.dougflutiejrfoundation.org.

Unlocking Autism — Call 1-866-366-3361 or visit www.unlockingautism.org/main.asp.